rep

ISSUE 02: GENE EDITING

rep

This issue
is about
Gene Editing!

ISSUE 02

Gene Editing

Welcome to rep.

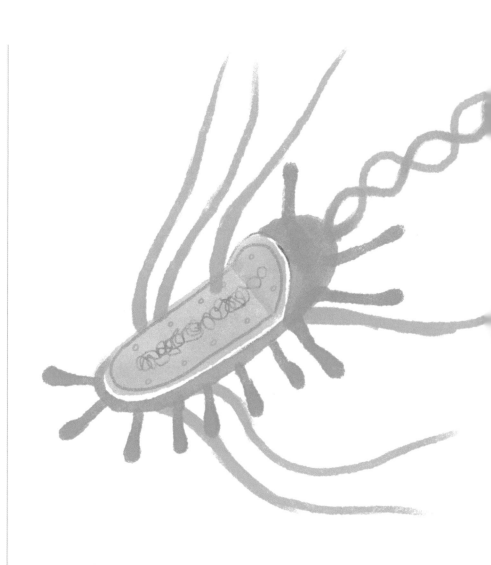

Credits

Lead Issue Learning Designer:
Karen Ingram

Rep Content Team:
Isabel Huff
Ariam Mogos
Megan Stariha
Carissa Carter
Laura McBain

Creative Direction + Visual Design:
Daniel Frumhoff

Cover Art:
Krista Franklin

Illustration:
Rashin Kheiriyeh

Technical Advisor:
Megan Palmer

This publication uses typeface families **Ginto** and **Ginto Nord** by the Dinamo Type Foundry.

Repmag.org
Creative Commons

All of the work we do is a collective effort and made possible by the d.school team, our teaching community, and the students we serve.

d.
HASSO PLATTNER
Institute of Design at Stanford

Gene editing surrounds us—and scientists have been doing it for a long time! There are new ways to use gene editing every day, but very few of us understand how it works. This issue is geared toward helping you understand how gene editing affects our lives and how you can become a designer of gene editing and other emerging (new) technologies like it, shaping the world around us.

Technology is power. As we create, we use that power, and it's important to consider the effects of what we design on others—people who might be different than us, children of the future, and the planet itself. We all have the right to understand, create, and design with technologies that will help the world become a better place for everyone.

Rep stands for a lot of important ideas: represent, reputation, repurpose, repower, and more. It is a symbol for our hope in the representative power of technology. It is our belief that when everyone is **rep**resented through design work, we can repair many of the world's broken systems.

Welcome to Rep.

Table of Contents

1

2

3

Products

4

Systems

5

Art Remix

Emerging technologies share a common framework, and can be prodded, pondered, poked and packaged through a few perspectives.

Our map will explore:

 Grab a pencil, you'll need it!

 Circle the response that feels correct!

 Time to reflect!

 Grab your scissors, you'll need them!

This is Design Work

Implications

Positive + Negative. Predicted + Unexpected.

What are the 2nd, 3rd...nth order effects of what we put into the world? For health? Safety? Society? Humanity? Earth? Are there ethical considerations to our creations?

Systems

Platforms + Movements.
Schools + Governments.

How do we create for multiple stakeholders with different, context-specific needs?

Experiences

Events + Spaces.
Moments + Feelings.

How do we design towards equity? Who are we excluding? Are humans at the center of our work? Should they be?

Products

Digital + Physical.
Form + Function.

Is everything created with intention? Are we considering the life of the product beyond its intended use? What expertise is needed to craft our designs?

Technologies

Emerging + Exponential.
Standalone + Leveraged.

Are we actively prototyping with AI, ML, blockchain, XR, biotech? Are we contributing to their development as well as their use?

Data

Sources + Algorithms.
Big + Small.

Is our data biased? Where is it from? Are we considering the balance between privacy and mass surveillance in our collection of it?

Introduction

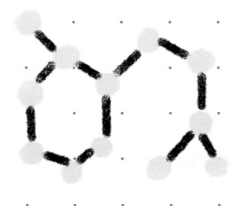

The field of gene editing is vast and rapidly expanding.

From new vaccines, to specialty crops, to new gene therapies, there's a lot to talk about! We're going to begin to explore the complexities of this emerging technology through the story of domestication—that is, how humans slowly created cattle that were gentle beings rather than wild animals.

People think gene editing is a new technology, but it has actually been happening for a long time. Now, people are applying gene editing to different big challenges.

Gene Editing: Past and Present

Thousands of years ago, humans began to domesticate plants and animals. Domesticating means humans chose specific plants or animals to reproduce for specific traits—like veggies that grew bigger, or cows that produced more milk.

Gene editing is a new way to do something humans have been doing for millennia. This timeline shows some of what came before gene editing, like events about animal and plant domestication. It also shows more recent events that relate to gene editing.

1997

Humans figure out the genes for a type of bacteria that lives in the human gut called E.Coli.

11,500 years ago

Humans begin to understand how to grow and harvest specific plants during different seasons to feed more people.

9,000 years ago

First evidence of fermentation in China (fruit, honey and rice).

1970s

Microbes (tiny living things) are engineered to produce human insulin (a chemical we need to survive).

10,500 years ago

Humans begin domesticating aurochs (Aw-raaks), which are the ancestors of some of our cattle today.

1627

The last auroch dies in Poland, making the auroch one of the first animal extinctions recorded.

1994

The first genetically modified organism (GMO), a tomato resistant to rotting, hits the grocery store.

13,000 years ago

Because they need food and companionship/help with hunting, humans begin to domesticate animals.

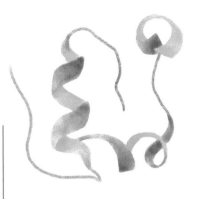

2015

The auroch genome is sequenced, meaning researchers can see its genes.

2015

Non-browning apples are ok'd for people to eat in the US and Canada.

2003

Glow-in-the-dark zebrafish are allowed to be sold in Taiwan, making them the first GMO pets.

2018

Golden Rice is ok'd for growing around the world.

2003

The first trials of "golden rice" begin. Golden rice has extra vitamins to prevent humans from going blind. At this time, it is made with genes from daffodils (a type of flower) and bacteria.

2015

The first genetically engineered hornless dairy cattle, two bulls named Buri and Spotigy, are born.

2019

Princess, a dairy cow genetically engineered to have no horns, is on the cover of a technology magazine.

Goal Cards

Gene editing could be used to help achieve the goals on these cards. Which ones do you most want to see happen?

Grab your scissors, you'll need them! Cut out the cards on the following pages.

Air Quality

Conservation

Climate Change

Pollution

Conservation

Protecting plants, animals, and their habitats (including the land).

Example Challenge:
Create new products that are biodegradable and reduce the use of single-use plastics (which injure and hurt wildlife).

Air Quality

Making sure air is safe and healthy to breathe.

Example Challenge:
Create new kinds of fuels that mean cars don't make the air as dirty.

Pollution

Getting rid of poisonous elements in the environment that could hurt people or other plants and animals.

Example Challenge:
Create new ways of fertilizing (feeding) plants that don't pollute rivers and streams.

Climate Change

Addressing some of the effects of shifts in climate.

Example Challenge:
Create new building materials that help protect homes when extreme hurricanes happen.

Saving Culture

Health

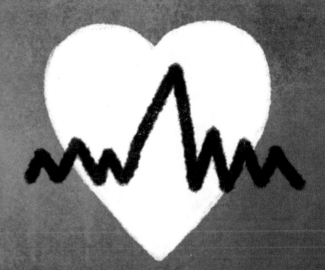

Food

Pest Control

Health

Designing better ways of preventing and treating health conditions.

Example Challenge:
Create new vaccines to make sure people don't get as sick from certain illnesses.

Saving Culture

Making sure a group of people's art, traditions, or history are not lost.

Example Challenge:
Bringing back an extinct plant or animal that was important to a specific group of people for cultural reasons.

Pest Control

Managing a plant or animal that could harm humans or the ecosystem.

Example Challenge:
Create new ways to prevent termites from destroying the foundations of houses and other buildings.

Food

Making sure all people have safe food and the nutrients (like vitamins) they need to be healthy.

Example Challenge:
Create fruits and veggies that stay fresh longer, so they can be transported to people who need them, but who live in places where they can't be grown.

Please don't cut this part off.

Address a challenge

Place your
goal card here

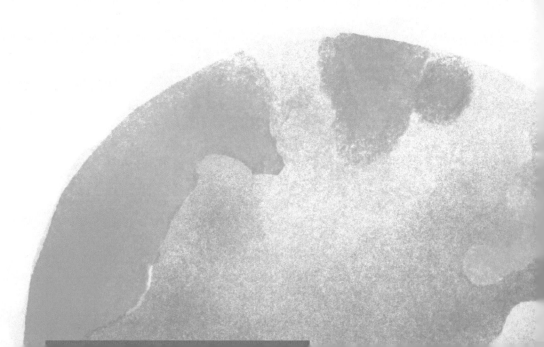

Look at the **goal cards**. Which one would you want to tackle? Place that card on the left page. Below, write about why you chose that card:

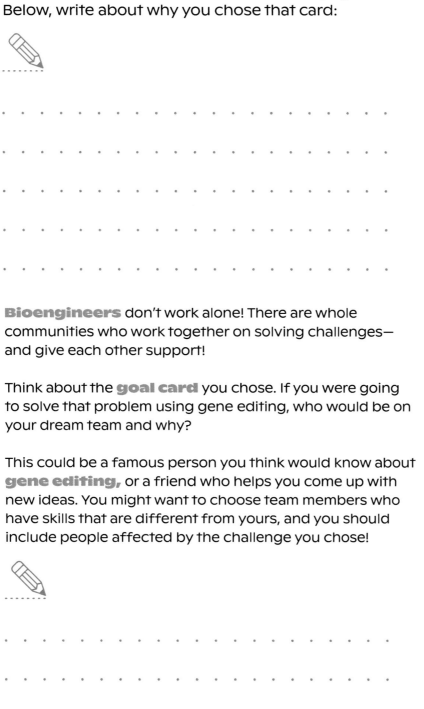

Bioengineers don't work alone! There are whole communities who work together on solving challenges— and give each other support!

Think about the **goal card** you chose. If you were going to solve that problem using gene editing, who would be on your dream team and why?

This could be a famous person you think would know about **gene editing,** or a friend who helps you come up with new ideas. You might want to choose team members who have skills that are different from yours, and you should include people affected by the challenge you chose!

Reflection

When you built your **dream team** on the previous page, did you put someone on your team who is directly affected by the challenge? How do you think having someone like that on your team would help **address your challenge?**

Technologies

Let's start with technologies

When we think of technology, we usually think of our phones and laptops, but technology also includes gene editing tools like **CRISPR** and **TALEN**, which give us the ability to change genetic material. Gene editing is a combination of many types of science and technologies to do and create new things.

The DNA of Your PB&J

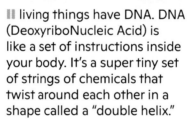

All living things have DNA. DNA (DeoxyriboNucleic Acid) is like a set of instructions inside your body. It's a super tiny set of strings of chemicals that twist around each other in a shape called a "double helix."

DNA tells different parts of your body what to do or make, almost like a recipe.

DNA tells your body to create skin, or hair, or lungs. It tells your body to make your eyes a certain color.

Bioengineers change the DNA instructions. It's kind of like taking a recipe—let's say, for a peanut butter sandwich—and making changes. If you change the instructions from "cut into triangles" to "cut into rectangles," the finished sandwich will look different.

Buri and Spotigy

Two cows engineered to not have horns.

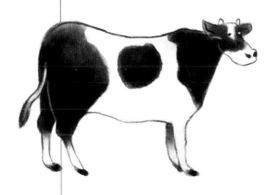

Let's take a look at a real–life example. Over hundreds of years, cattle that have been chosen for better meat (beef cattle) are different from cattle that have been chosen for better milk (dairy cattle). It just so happens that dairy cattle have horns, whereas some beef cattle do not. Dairy farmers often remove the dairy cow's horns so the cows don't hurt people or each other. Removing the horns is stressful for the cow as well as the person doing it.

Wouldn't it be great if we could give dairy cattle the genes beef cattle have to stop horns from growing? That's what bioengineers did with two dairy cattle named Buri and Spotigy— they took their DNA instructions and changed them from "create horns" to "don't create horns." How? One way bioengineers work is by taking a set of instructions from one living thing and putting them into another living thing.

Let's think about the sandwich example again. Pretend you wanted to create a recipe for a peanut butter only sandwich. Instead of writing the entire recipe from the beginning, you could copy the part of a PB&J recipe that tells the cook how to spread the peanut butter onto the bread.

Recipe DNA

S why haven't you had a milkshake, ice cream, or yogurt from hornless dairy cattle? Even though researchers created dairy cattle with no horns, there was a little hiccup.

Two parts of our government— the Food and Drug Administration (FDA) and the United States Department of Agriculture (USDA) —have the job of keeping us safe and our food safe. The USDA thought the new cattle were okay, but the FDA discovered something different.

The researchers provided the USDA and the FDA with the hornless cow's DNA, and the FDA noticed that there was some DNA that was extra in the cattle—it wasn't part of the "don't make horns" instructions.

The FDA knew that the researchers hadn't specifically wanted that extra DNA in there. While it wasn't necessarily good or bad, there was no way to know how it would affect the cattle or people eating products from the cow.

Sort of like if you used a pen to write your new peanut–butter–only sandwich, but the pen left an ink blot. The ink blot wouldn't necessarily be bad for or affect your sandwich, but it could confuse the sandwich maker if it made some words hard to read (or made them look like different words!). Peanut butt? Peanut butter? Peanut butterfly? Peanut button? Peanuts don't have butts, there's no such thing as a peanut butterfly, and a button shaped like a peanut wouldn't be very tasty. We could assume that it's peanut butter and the extra ink blot is nothing to worry about, but can we be 100% sure? The FDA didn't think so.

So, that meant "try again" for the hornless cattle.

Attributes, Parts, and Behaviors

When we create recipes in gene editing, we make those recipes with attributes, parts, and behaviors. What are the attributes, parts, and behaviors of cows we have now?

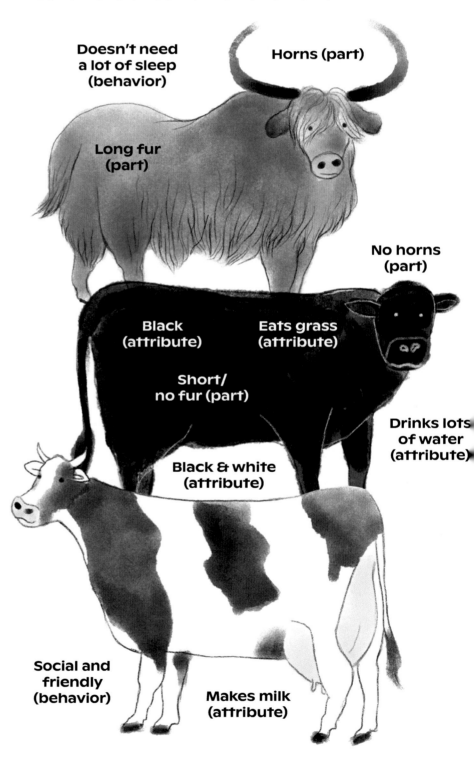

Doesn't need a lot of sleep (behavior)

Horns (part)

Long fur (part)

No horns (part)

Black (attribute)

Eats grass (attribute)

Short/ no fur (part)

Drinks lots of water (attribute)

Black & white (attribute)

Social and friendly (behavior)

Makes milk (attribute)

What are some attributes, parts and, behaviors that people might use gene editing to create in the future?

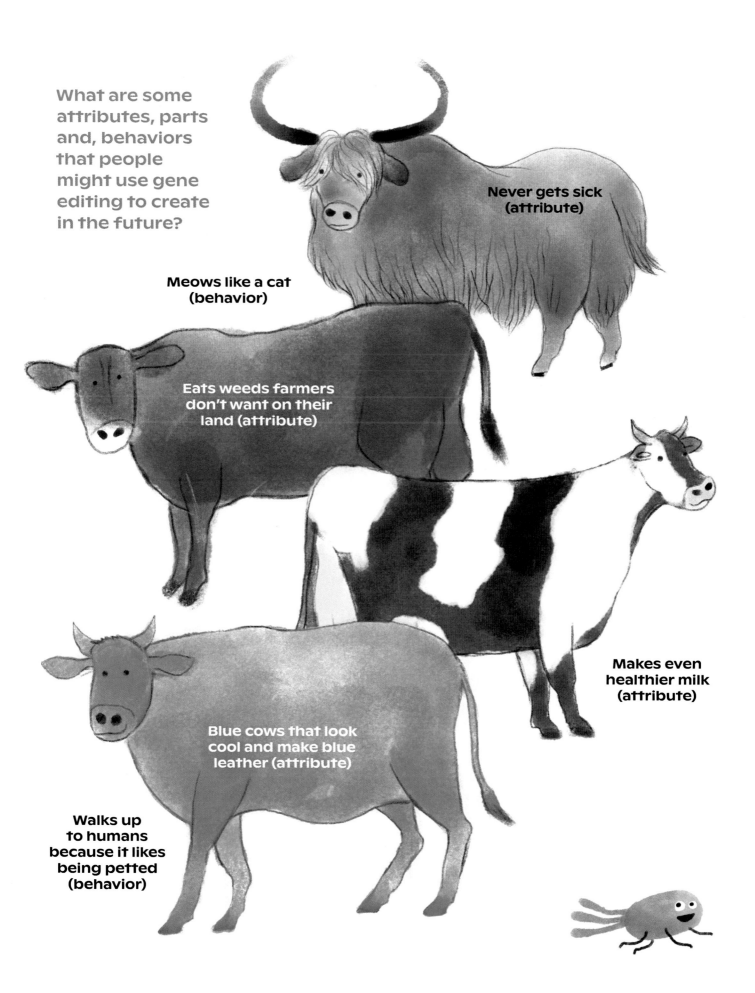

Never gets sick (attribute)

Meows like a cat (behavior)

Eats weeds farmers don't want on their land (attribute)

Makes even healthier milk (attribute)

Blue cows that look cool and make blue leather (attribute)

Walks up to humans because it likes being petted (behavior)

For each challenge below, figure out which **attribute**, **part**, or **behavior** you would change with gene editing to solve the problem. Then, draw your solution!

Try it out

Problems

This cow is **sweating** because it lives at a farm where it's really hot.

In some environments, **Japanese Honeysuckle** can be harmful to other plants because it uses a lot of water and sun that other plants need too.

flies around

bites humans

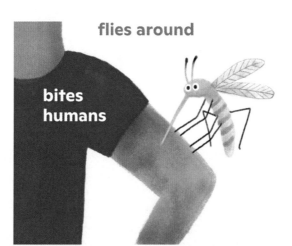

Mosquitos fly around and bite humans, which can spread **sicknesses**.

Solutions

What part of the cow could you change to help it be less hot?

Draw it:

· · · · · · · · · · · · · · · · · · · ·

· · · · · · · · · · · · · · · · · · · ·

· · · · · · · · · · · · · · · · · · · ·

What attribute of the Japanese Honeysuckle could you change to make it kill fewer other plants?

Draw it:

· · · · · · · · · · · · · · · · · · · ·

· · · · · · · · · · · · · · · · · · · ·

· · · · · · · · · · · · · · · · · · · ·

What behavior of the mosquito could you change to make sure it doesn't spread sicknesses to humans?

Draw it:

· · · · · · · · · · · · · · · · · · · ·

· · · · · · · · · · · · · · · · · · · ·

· · · · · · · · · · · · · · · · · · · ·

Reflection

Choose another **goal card** with a challenge you would want to address. Put it below:

**Place your
goal card here**

What living things are part of this challenge?

What parts, attributes, or behaviors of those living things could you change with gene editing to help solve this challenge?

Is it possible to address this challenge without gene editing? Does gene editing provide specific benefits? (If not, that's ok!)

Draw It

Products

What Products Are Made with Gene Editing?

We continue our journey with gene editing by looking at how it's used to create different types of products.

Products are digital, physical and living things that people create to meet a need or solve a problem.

**Grab a pencil,
you'll need it!**

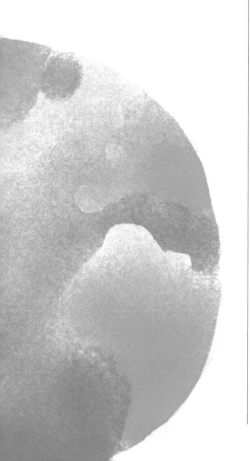

What Products Can Be Made with Gene Editing?

Gene editing is a field focused on changing organisms (living things) to have new traits or abilities. Engineers read and write DNA (deoxyribonucleic acid) to get to those traits and abilities. We'll expand more on what that means later.

What features or abilities would we want in an organism? Well, that depends on the organism, and it depends on the goal!

Gene editing can be used to make products that address the challenges and goals you read about in the previous section! Right now, scientists and engineers are using gene editing technologies to create all kinds of products, including:

• Foods that stay fresh longer, foods that contain extra vitamins and nutrients that humans need, or ways of farming that result in less chemical use

• More sustainable, renewable energy sources

• New products for health including vaccines and treatments

• New materials for clothing and construction

• New ways to address environmental challenges like extinction, trash, and pollution

And so much more, as we will see!

Apples have been made to bruise less, which means they stay fresh on the shelf longer.

Fish are made to glow using DNA from jellyfish and coral. Engineers created these fish to glow to tell them when certain toxins are in the water.

Gene editing was used to make COVID–19 vaccines.

Elizabeth Ann is an endangered black footed ferret brought to life with gene editing to help keep the species from going extinct.

The Darling 58, a type of American Chestnut tree, has been made to be blight resistant (that means it's harder for the tree to get a certain disease).

Spider silk is one of the strongest materials on earth, but it's very hard to harvest! So engineers used gene editing to make goats that produce spider silk protein in their milk. It's much easier to collect that way!

Why Use Gene Editing?

Gene editing is already helping us get things we need! Researchers are using microbes (tiny living things) like yeast and bacteria to make medicines, flavors, materials, and more:

WITHOUT gene editing

We have to use pig organs to get insulin, a chemical that people with diabetes need.

We have to buy vanilla from flowers in the island country of Madagascar, and it can cost a lot of money.

We could use spider silk! But we would have to farm spiders, which is impossible because they fight each other!

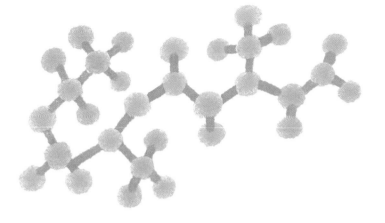

But WITH gene editing...

We can get microbes (tiny living things) to make insulin in a lab.

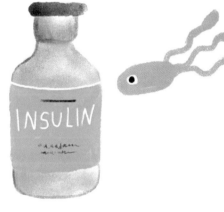

Getting insulin doesn't require using animals!

We can get yeast to make the vanilla flavor to put in our desserts.

Our vanilla desserts can be more affordable!

We can get yeast to make spider silk and spin it into fabric.

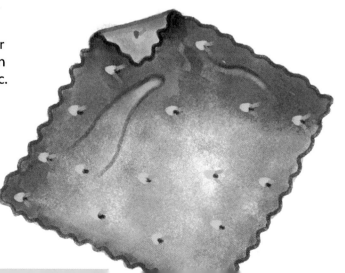

We can make fabric from spider silk, one of the strongest materials on earth!

Planning for the Long-term Future

What would a future with gene editing look like in the next 20, 50, or even 100 years? Some of these projects are actively being worked on, and some are not. What would you like to see? What would you NOT like to see? Who do you think would be helped and harmed by each idea? Add your ideas to the timeline!

2044
Because of gene edited mosquitoes, sicknesses like malaria (that mosquitoes had spread) are wiped out.

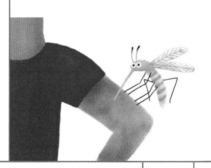

2062
Gene editing means we can quickly download medicine at home.

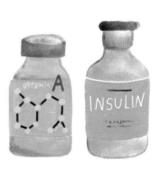

2042
The American Chestnut tree begins to grow well again in American forests!

2059
Almost all hamburger meat is made in labs instead of raising cattle.

2054

. . . .

. . . .

. . . .

Add your idea.
Fill in the spaces.

2084

. . . .
. . . .
. . . .
. . . .
. . . .
. . . .

2098
The woolly mammoth comes out of extinction and begins to live at the north pole.

2120
The first potatoes are grown on Mars, bringing Martian Potato chips to earthlings.

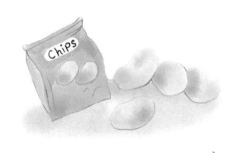

2094
People begin growing gardens with plants they can customize to fit their tastes.

2096
Glow-in-the-dark kittens become the most popular pet, leading to a surge in the mouse population because mice see the cats and avoid them easily.

2115
An amusement park filled with dinosaurs opens up on an island off the coast of Costa Rica.

2179
Through working with nature, we learn how to send messages via plant roots!

What could you create?

Choose an Organism:

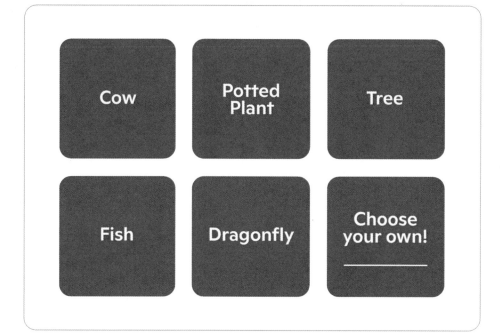

Cow	Potted Plant	Tree
Fish	Dragonfly	Choose your own! _____

Choose an Characteristic:

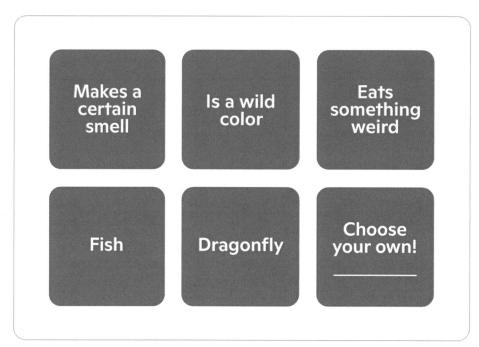

Makes a certain smell	Is a wild color	Eats something weird
Fish	Dragonfly	Choose your own! _____

Combine an **organism** and a **characteristic** with **gene editing** to make something new!

1. **What could you create?**

I'm designing a _____ that _____
(Organism)   (Characteristic)

2. **What problem/need could that solve?**

_____

_____

_____

3. **What problem could that create?**

_____

_____

_____

4. **Draw an ad for the product you could make from your combination!**

Reflection

Why do you think people use **gene editing** to make products?

Systems

What Systems Are Affected by Gene Editing?

Everything exists in a system made up of different parts that affect each other. It's important for us to understand how gene editing can have an impact on many types of systems.

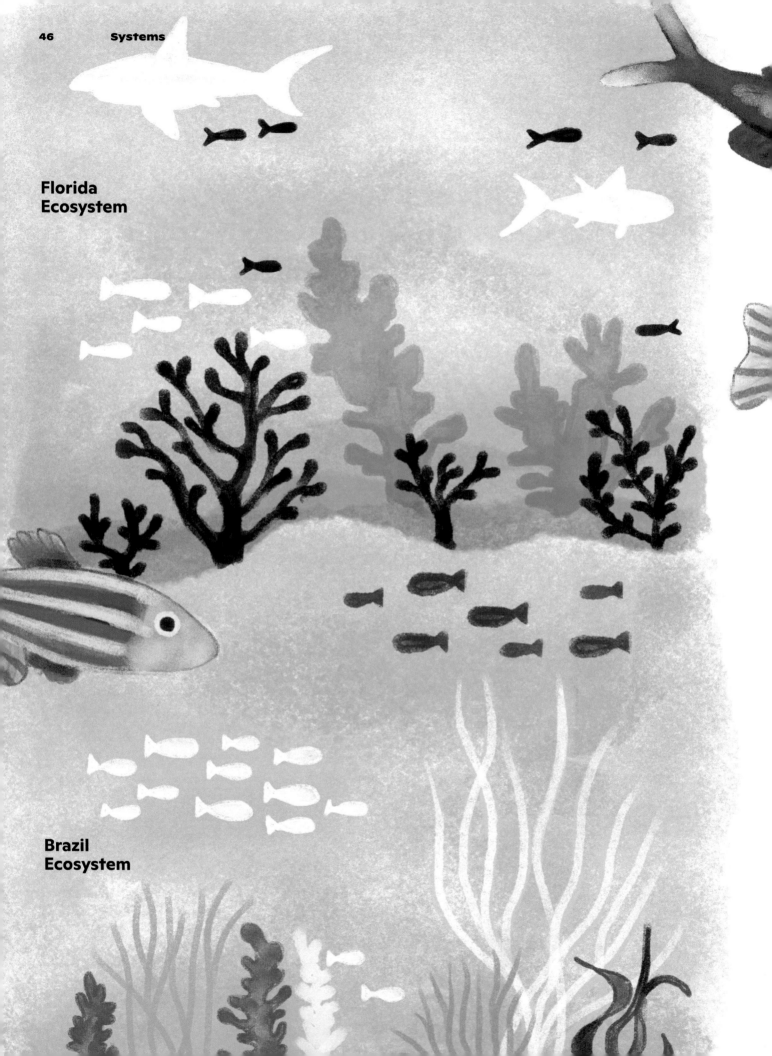

Florida
Ecosystem

Brazil
Ecosystem

A Glowing Fish Story

Meet the Zebrafish. The Zebrafish is a little striped fish that's a popular pet, swimming in aquariums all over the world. Scientists have been doing research with Zebrafish for several decades. The research they do is important for making new drugs for people and it's also important for the health of the environment. A research group in Singapore used gene editing to make Zebrafish that change color when there are certain bad toxins in water. The colors came from the DNA of deep sea creatures like jellyfish and coral. Because these fish were so popular anyway, a company decided to sell these extra bright Zebrafish in 2004 as pets in America, without the ability to tell if toxins were in the water. They were cool additions to black light aquariums because they glowed, and people made them in more and more dazzling colors. The fish soon found their way around the world, where they were raised and sold as pets. These fish were the very first gene edited pets.

In order to keep up with demand, the glowing fish were raised in fisheries around the world. A fishery is a special place where fish are raised for food or for pets. Sometimes fisheries are connected to larger bodies of water. In 2014, one glowing fish escaped from a fishery in Florida. It appeared this little fish got gulped down quickly because no one could find it. Research in 2011 had showed glowing fish were easy prey for larger fish in Florida, so they wouldn't find much of a home in Florida waters.

Sometimes when a living thing is brought into a new ecosystem and reproduces quickly, it might change the ecosystem. In 2015, the first glowing Zebrafish were spotted in a river in Brazil, having escaped from a hatchery. In 2022, the fish seemed to be doing well in the wild in Brazil. In this location (unlike Florida), these fish found a rich diet, could breed all year, and didn't have predators. These Zebrafish multiplied quickly and were spotted in many bodies of water, which might hurt the ecosystem in the future. The government then banned sales of the fish in Brazil, but the fish are already out there in the wild.

So, what's next? Gene edited cats to catch the gene edited fish? How would you stop this from happening next time? Or do you think it would happen no matter what and plan for it?

Systems

It's hard to know what the impacts of a design will be...

You're right! There might be something you don't think of. It also might take a lot of time or money to figure out what could go wrong with your design.

That's even **MORE** true when you realize how many types of systems there are! What we design can have an impact on not just one system, but many kinds. Here's just a few:

1

Ecosystem

The ecosystem is the community of living things around us. It includes plants, animals, microbes, people, as well as natural elements, like water and soil. As we design, it's important to consider how our design might impact the ecosystem we place it in. Some examples of ecosystems are forest, grassland, and desert, and even ecosystems on other planets! **(We saw the impact the Zebrafish had on the marine ecosystem!)**.

2

Research and Development (R&D)

In the research and development system, we think about what we'd like to design, what resources (like time, money, materials, and knowledge) we have, and how we are going to design it. The R&D system is about bringing our ideas to life and seeing if they work as we expect. Scientists and researchers are part of that system.

3

Production and Distribution systems

After we've made a design that we like, we have to make (or "produce") a bunch of them! Once our design is produced, how do we get our design into the hands of those who need it? (For example, from the factory to your house). That's what distribution systems are for.

which system?

Think about the story of the Glowing Zebrafish. Which systems were affected in the story?

Which system is this? Remember systems overlap, so you can circle more than one!

1. **Fisheries that grow the fish**

   (R&D) | Ecosystem | (Production and Distribution)

2. **Other fish and plants in the ocean**

   R&D | Ecosystem | Production and Distribution

3. **Pet stores that sell the fish**

   R&D | Ecosystem | Production and Distribution

4. **The bioengineers who used gene editing to create the fish that glow**

   R&D | Ecosystem | Production and Distribution

5. **Biologists in Florida & Brazil**

   R&D | Ecosystem | Production and Distribution

A System that Helps Us

hoa. So you have to think about how your design could affect ALL of those systems! But what if you miss something? And what about designers who want to make money and aren't as worried about how their designs could impact those systems?

Luckily, there's actually a system that helps with that! It's called the regulatory system, and you've actually already heard a bit about it.

The **FDA** and **USDA** are two groups that are part of the regulatory system. The point of the regulatory system is to make rules that help keep all the other systems (and us!) safe. They make sure designers are following the rules and help figure out what impacts a new design could have.

Remember Buri and Spotigy, the dairy cattle that didn't have horns? You learned how two parts of our government, the Food and Drug Administration (FDA) and the United States Department of Agriculture (USDA) had to approve Buri and Spotigy before any of their potential offspring could make dairy products for us.

What could Go Wrong/Right?

Imagine it's 2050! There's so much we can do with gene editing now! Three unique cows have been designed with gene editing, and they are having different impacts on different systems. Can you figure out how the cows are impacting these different systems?

This is a **purple cow**. People used gene editing to create it because they were bored with regular cows. What do you think that could mean for other systems?

Hint: we did SOME of the Purple Cow's effects for you, but there are more! Each cow can have multiple effects on systems, and some effects could be caused by multiple cows!

Effects

Production and Distribution: A small group of people really want purple leather, so a few select farms start raising these cows.

Production and Distribution: People don't like that gene editing was used just to change the way these cows look, especially when gene editing comes with some risks to the cows. They refuse to buy ANY products made from these cows. As a result, only a few farms choose to raise these cows.

Production and Distribution: Farmers stop using prairie land to grow hay, and instead buy algae and seaweed from people who grow or harvest those plants.

Instructions: Draw lines between the cows and the impacts they are having on different systems. (Hint: One cow can have multiple effects, and some effects could be caused by multiple cows!)

This cow **doesn't burp or fart**—which means it produces less methane and contributes less to climate change. What do you think that could mean for **different systems**?

This cow **eats algae and seaweed** instead of grass. Those plants take less resources to grow. What do you think that could mean for **different systems**?

Production and Distribution: These cows are easier for certain pests to see, which means they get more fly bites and the population of flies goes up. That's bad for all nearby cow farmers, because their cows start getting more bites too.

Ecosystem: Although the human population is growing and humans are still eating meat, the air is cleaner and cows are not making climate change worse.

Ecosystem: Ponds start becoming healthier because over-growth of algae is being removed.

R&D: Researchers use what they've learned with these cows to see if they can make similar changes to other livestock animals to combat climate change.

R&D: While the goal was just to make the cow eat seaweed, some other genes were accidentally edited and they made the cow have only one horn.

Grab a pencil, you'll need it!

Dinos of the Future?!

People find a way to use **gene editing** to bring back a dinosaur from the past. Specifically, they choose the dinosaur that eventually became our modern–day chicken! Here are some things that could happen next:

1. People start hunting the dinosaurs, and they become popular for fine dining. No one wants chickens anymore. This could impact the **production and distribution system**, specifically **chicken farmers**. They would be impacted because:

   _____

   If people want to eat dinosaurs instead of chicken, how would that affect the farmers who raise and sell chickens for people to eat?

   but, it would help if _____
   (What could the farmers do to deal with the impact?)

   _____

   _____

2. The dinosaurs start killing and eating insects and small rodents, like rabbits and rats. This could impact the _____ system,
   (What system are the hawks and rodents part of?)

   specifically **hawks**. They would be impacted because **they depend on rodents and insects for their food too, and because the dinosaurs are eating them, there aren't enough**. One way to help would be:

   _____

   _____

   _____

   (What could humans do to make sure there is enough for the hawks to eat? There are multiple possible answers! Think about how humans could make sure the dinos don't eat all of the wild rodents, OR how humans could make sure the hawks get enough to eat).

3. All of the dinosaurs start dying from a new disease. This would mostly impact the dinosaurs, but **scientists**, who are part of the _____ system, want to help.

(What system are scientists/researchers part of?)

In order to help the dinosaurs, the scientists could research:

_____

_____

_____

(What could the scientists do or figure out to help the dinosaurs?)

Reflection

Why is it important that we think about **systems** and not just the specific thing we're creating with **gene editing?**

Art Remix

Create your vision of our future with gene editing!

What possible futures could exist if we released new gene edited cows onto planet Earth right now?

Artist Statement:

Krista Franklin

My work emerges at the intersection of poetics, pop culture, and the dynamic histories of the African Diaspora. The Fantastic, the surreal, myth-making, and portraiture are preoccupations in my work. The forms take shape in collage, hand paper-making, installation, poetry, bookmaking, and performance.

I appropriate image and text as political gesture; to chisel away at narratives historically inscribed on Black women, femmes, and other people of color, to forge imaginative spaces for radical possibilities and visions. I orchestrate the collision of the past, the present and the future, and my fictional and historical memory for artistic content.

The collective and collaborative are also central to my work. I cultivate artistic community with fellow artists, writers and scholars. It is a vital practice for me, and a continuous undercurrent that fosters the advancement of creative liberation, reflection, scholarship, and artistic communion.

Go to the next page to build your vision of gene editing.

Artists help us imagine new worlds — or the future of our own world — that we haven't seen yet. In this issue, you learned a lot about gene editing. Now it's your turn to create your vision of our future with gene editing using Krista Franklin's drawings!

Use these clippings to design your own cow. How might you change or improve it?

1. Select a sky backdrop for a background, or find a photo of your own to use!

2. Cut out your favorite elements from Franklin's work, compiled across the following pages.

3. Arrange cut-out elements over the background to make a remixed collage.

Cut to Remix!

**Grab your scissors,
you'll need them!**

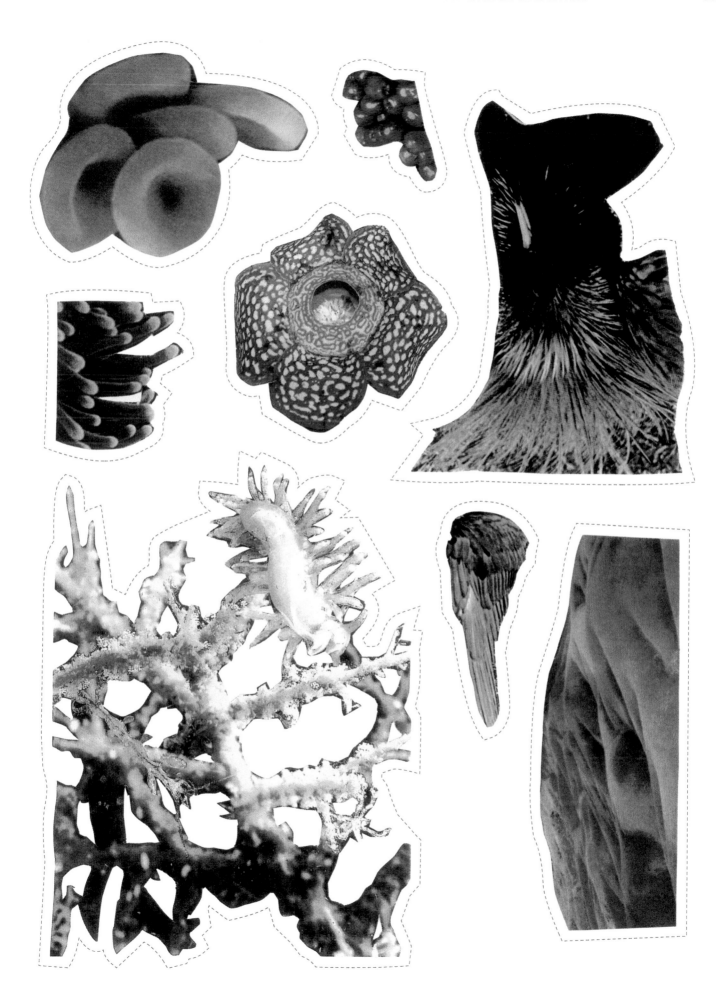

cut to Remix!

**Grab your scissors,
you'll need them!**

cut to Remix!

**Grab your scissors,
you'll need them!**

rep

rep

rep

repair

repair

represent

repower

represent

repower   rep

reputation

repair   reputation

cut to Remix!

Grab your scissors, you'll need them!

cut to Remix!

**Grab your scissors,
you'll need them!**

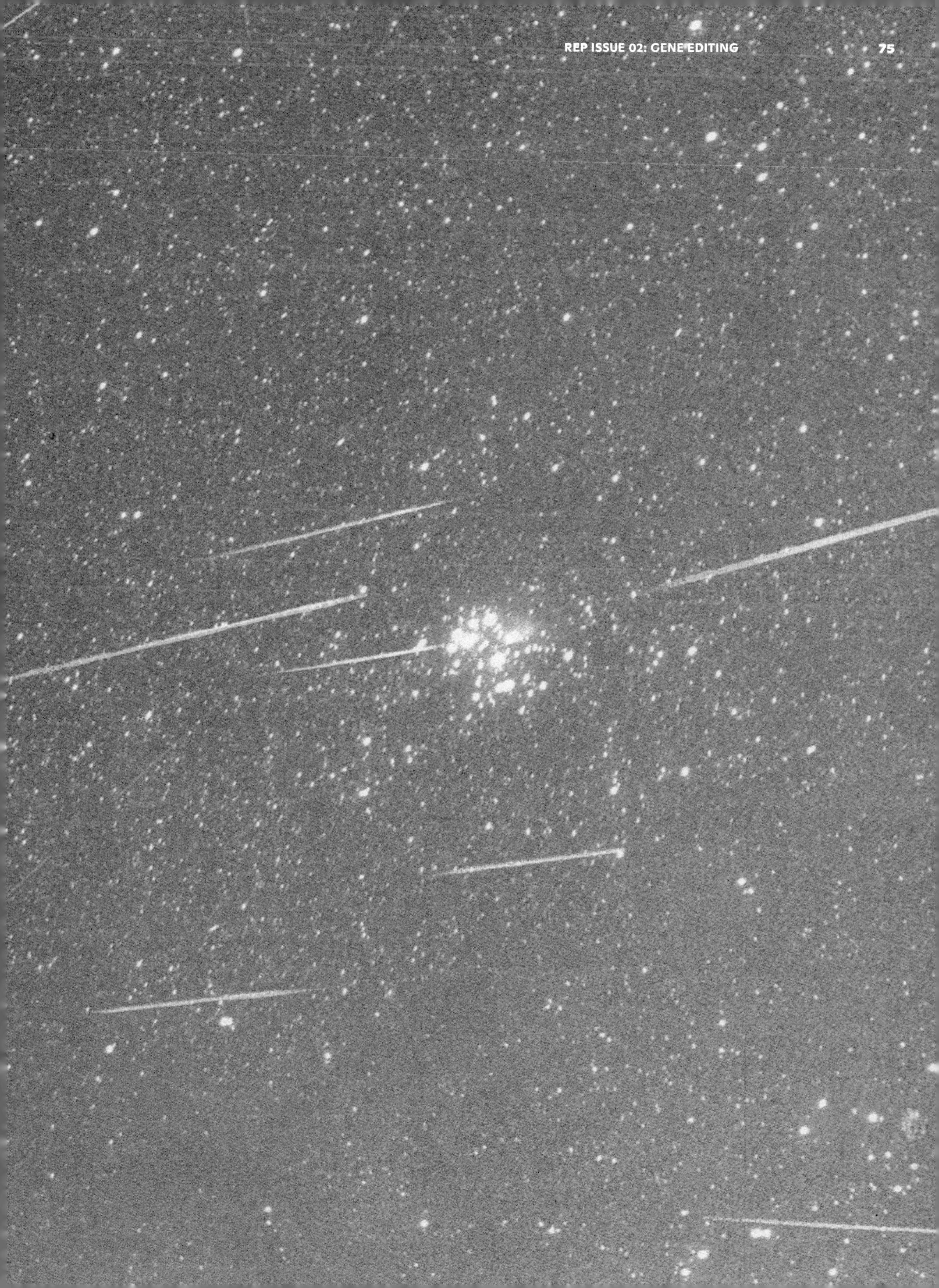

Gene Editing: Key Terms

DNA (deoxyribonucleic acid) Chemical instructions that tell parts of our body what to do. Small parts of DNA are called genes.

Domestication Changes that happen in wild animals or plants when they are grown and raised by humans. The changes are often made by humans over many decades.

Gene editing (also called "genetic engineering" and "genetic modification"): Making a change to a plant, animal, or micro-organism by changing its DNA instructions.

Gene sequence The order that genes follow to create a specific plant, animal, or micro-organism's DNA. When a living thing is sequenced and compared to another living thing, we can see the similarities and differences (from their instructions).

Genome The whole set of genes for a specific organism.

Microbes A tiny organism (living thing) like bacteria or yeast.

Organism A living thing. Organisms include plants, animals, bacteria, yeast, and more.

Notes

rep|